IMAGES
of America

ST. LOUIS
UNION STATION

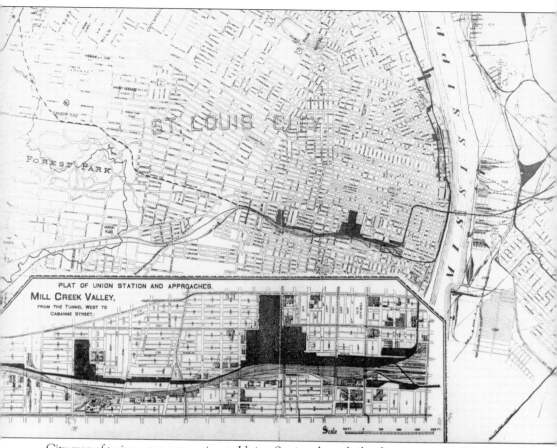

City map of train routes connecting to Union Station through the then existing Mill Creek Valley.

IMAGES
of America

St. Louis
Union Station

Albert Montesi and Richard Deposki

ARCADIA

Published by Arcadia Publishing
Charleston SC, Chicago IL, Portsmouth NH, San Francisco CA

Printed in Great Britain

Library of Congress Catalog Card Number: 2002104385

For all general information contact Arcadia Publishing at:
Telephone 843-853-2070
Fax 843-853-0044
E-Mail sales@arcadiapublishing.com

For customer service and orders:
Toll-Free 1-888-313-2665

Visit us on the internet at http://www.arcadiapublishing.com

Union Station at the turn of the twentieth century.

CONTENTS

Acknowledgments   6

Introduction   7

1.   Beginnings   9

2.   Union Station   15

3.   The Midway   31

4.   Train Shed, Yards, and Trains   41

5.   Grand Hall   57

6.   Dining and Other Facilities   63

7.   Operations   71

8.   Suburban Stations and Other Railway Connections   75

9.   Postcards   93

10.   Decline and a New Beginning   101

11.   Renovated Facilities and Amusements   107

12.   "A New Life Springs"   121

Bibliography   128

ACKNOWLEDGMENTS

The authors would like to acknowledge the following:

Meramec Valley Historical Society
Webster-Kirkwood Times, Inc. (DwightBitikofer)
Charles Guenther
St. Louis Union Station
Willis Goldschmidt
Walter Eschbach
Malcolm C. Drummond
Richard Gruss
Kirkwood Historical Society
Ferguson Historical Society (Ruth Brown)

Special thanks to:
Skip Gatermann
Missouri Botanical Garden
Special Collections, St. Louis Public Library
    (Jean E. Meeh Gosebrink)
Fine Arts Department (Mary S. Enns Frechette)
Jennifer L. Rawlings
Innovations for Kitchen & Bath
Jefferson Camera Shop
Lonnie Tettaton

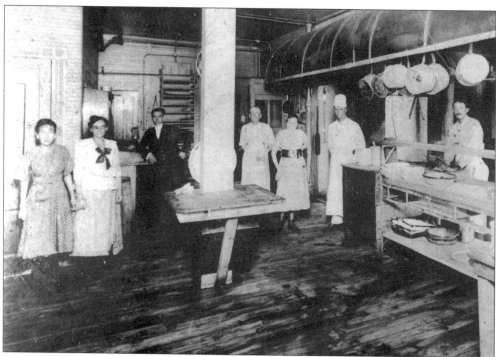

Pictured is a kitchen that prepared food to be served on trains.

INTRODUCTION

St. Louis' industrial growth and its coming of age as an urban commercial power in the nineteenth century was nothing short of phenomenal. From its very beginning, it was sought out as a trading center for its economic potential. Its position near the confluence of the Mississippi and Missouri rivers provided an ideal locale for transportation and shipping. It is not surprising, then, that as the Midwest grew in population and region, the city grew with it. Early in the century, as steam and water power became new sources of marine energy, St. Louis prospered as steamboats crowded its wharfs. As the century grew older, however, new technology provided the times with a new player, the railroads, which, unlike the steamboat, could fan out into the new opening West.

Before and particularly after the Civil War, railcars and their tracks began to appear throughout the United States in great numbers. As the steamboat era declined, St. Louis (in rivalry with Chicago) realized that it must build some method of crossing the Mississippi to accommodate the tracks that were needed.

This was solved by the engineering genius of James B. Eads who performed a feat seemingly impossible for the day. He spanned the Mississippi River with a crossing buttressed by pylons dug deep in the wide river. In 1874, he presented the city with the famous Eads Bridge, an engineering and aesthetic triumph that stunned the nation and provided the city with the necessary means to competitively enter the grand "Age of the Railroad."

Though successful in the beginning, the Eads Bridge Company became enmeshed in a political rivalry with the barge owners who, before the bridge was built, had carted all trains across the river. In time, the company encountered financial difficulties and soon fell into the hands of the masterful entrepreneur, Jay Gould, who controlled most of the country's new railroads. Gould charged exorbitant prices for trains other than his own to use the bridge's tracks.

Jay Gould later lost control of his great Middle West train empire and turned over all of his holdings to his son and heir, as well as to William Taussig, a close associate. These two men then formed a joint-holding company, which in time included various railroad companies and their routes and carriers. Thus was born the very important venture that was known as the Terminal Railroad Association.

In the meanwhile, the first major train station in the city, erected in downtown St. Louis, became inadequate as train traffic grew enormously. Taussig, the sagacious head of the Terminal group, together with his associates, began to plan for a larger and more attractive venue. In keeping with the architectural trend of the day, railroad stations were built in urban centers with grandiose designs and construction. Taussig wished to rival those in New York, Boston, and Washington with the most elaborate and graceful structure of them all.

Prominent local architect Theodore Link won the design contest and patterned the station after a walled city in Carcassonne, France. Reining in the best talent in sculpture, stained-glass window design, and interior decoration, Link created a masterful railroad station whose technical ingenuity and operational engineering matched in some fortunate coordination the aesthetic beauty and graceful contours of its whole.

This Richardsonian Romanesque structure, called Union Station, soon became a beehive of activity as it evolved into a railroad center to which most of the nation traveled. It grew in time to be one of the busiest stations in the world.

Yet as the twentieth century saw technological inventions and advances in transportation, Union Station became threatened by the new times. As the motorcar and airplane opened up new modes of transportation, the railroads suffered. They suffered to such a degree that Union Station became more and more idle. The vast hordes that once walked its floors became almost nonexistent. In time, the station closed. Now forsaken, it fell prey to vandals and thieves, its lovely features gutted and destroyed. Soon it sat empty, an ugly shell, disabled and forlorn for decades.

In 1985, its status fortunately changed as a $150 million restoration took place. Artists and artisans made painstaking efforts to restore it to its original brilliant shape. It has since become a vast entertainment center with shops, restaurants, amusements, and a grand hotel: a site that attracts as many as 5 million visitors a year.

In the following pages, we have attempted to capture, with photos and commentary, the rise, decline, and final restoration of this grand structure.

Rail workers "bum" a ride on a railroad tractor at the turn of the twentieth century. (Special Collections, St. Louis Public Library.)

One

BEGINNINGS

Several early railroads served the St. Louis area before the opening of the first substantial rail station, the Old St. Louis Union Depot between Ninth and Twelfth in 1874. Among these were the Pacific, the St. Louis Iron Mountain, and the North Missouri railroads. These had stops in the city at Fourteenth Street near Poplar in the old Mill Creek area; at the west side of Seventh Street at Poplar; and at Main and Plum Streets.

One of the earliest was built in Ferguson. Here we see a steam-propelled early model of a giant engine puffing into the Ferguson Station. Previously, Ferguson provided the first track ever made by a railroad to and from St. Louis. (Ferguson Historical Society.)

Here we see the old Ferguson Station itself, built before 1885. (Ferguson Historical Society.)

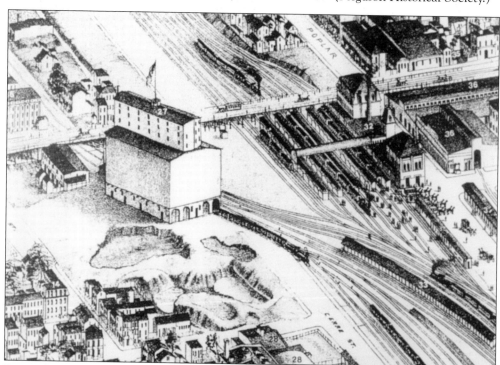

Pictured is a Compton and Dry drawing of the Old St. Louis Union Depot. It contained an 11 track arrangement, with railroad offices on the second floor. Built of stone and brick, it was a definite improvement over the wooden, shed-like structures that had previously served the trains entering the city.

The Union Depot served St. Louis before the construction of Union Station.

Here is another view of the Old Depot, which in less than ten years, became outmoded. Its traffic soared as America entered the "Age of the Railroad."

The train yards of the Depot house, a state-of-the art engine of its day with the funnel-like smoke stack. (St. Louis Public Library.)

A St. Louis and Iron Mountain Railroad station stands at Itaska Street in South St. Louis. It was necessary to mount the station high on the bluffs to meet the level of the street and then add a long staircase to enter the train below. This is one of the pre-Depot stations in a photo taken before the Civil War. (St. Louis and Iron Mountain and Southern Railroad.)

Another early train station at Jefferson Barracks served the St. Louis Iron Mountain and Southern railway system, c. 1890. (St. Louis Public Library.)

Two

UNION STATION

As we have seen, with the St. Louis Depot becoming too small and with the creation of the St. Louis Terminal Company, William Taussig and his associates wished to create a railroad station that was a work of monumental authority and beauty, a work of art as well as a practical building. Plans for the new station were in the offing years ahead of its final completion. Finally in 1894, the massive, medieval-like building came into being. In attempting to delineate its life and times, we have selected lines from "Union Station," a poem by the famed local poet Charles Guenther, whose lines lyrically capture the history of this historical building. Guenther starts his poem exploring the geological, pre-historic earth upon which the station now stands. In the next stanza, the poem describes the land when it was open and free, when only Native Americans and buffalo roamed upon it. The poem then narrates how the land becomes part of the growing new city, a part of the damned-up streams that make up Mill Creek. Next, our poet tells how the creek is expanded to create the famed Chouteau's Pond, which in turn is drained and covered over to become the site of many local businesses. In time, these buildings were demolished to provide the station with its site and center. Then the poem marks the railway structure's decline and finally, the long period when it lie broken and vandalized—a shabby relic of its grand past self. The last lines, as we shall see, sing of its new life after its restoration.

Pictured here is Chouteau's Mill in 1850, at what is now Fifth and Poplar. (St. Louis Public Library.)

15

UNION STATION
by Charles Guenther

Only the swallows circling these cones of silence
Make this their hostel now. Their invisible track
Circumscribes a valley where ancient springs
Flowed from the western hills before the air
Droned with wheels by the dam and the artificial pool
In the mills that stood near the gorge where Rock Creek ends.

Theodore Link, the celebrated Missouri architect, submitted the winning design for the new station. Here we see a late-1800s photograph of the distinguished artist who was the guiding figure responsible for not only the building's exterior, but also the majestic design of its interior. Link provided the new station with its excellent operational aptitude through enormous engineering savvy, as illustrated here. These are the tracks by which the railcars entered the train shed.

How the face of the valley changes! One thing ends,
Replaced by another with intervals of silence:
Once there was a prairie with scrub oak, an occasional pool
Where buffalo grazed and drank their rumbling track
Mistaken for thunder shook the morning air.
Flushing out every creature that flies or springs.

The *prairie with scrub oak* becomes the train yards of the new structure.

Passengers entered their railcars in the train shed, the building into which these tracks run.

Yet who knows how many thousands of springs
The same scenario plays before it ends,
How many upheavals of earth and air
Hold no recollection in postludes of silence:
Only a beetle perhaps, inscribing its track
Patiently, returns to the edge of an obscure pool.

And here the Osage camped where the bed of the pool
Lay, settlers came for the pure springs
And the black earth, mountain men left to track
Deer and beaver from where the Missouri ends
Up to its headwaters in the lands of silence,
And boatmen labored and danced to some old French air.

Here is another view of the tracks as they flow into the glass and steel train shed. (St. Louis Public Library.)

17

Under cedars and cottonwoods, ghosts in the moonlit air.
Lovers pressed on the grass the glassy pool
(Where have they gone? Only a winter silence
Lies with the faded stones by the vanished springs).
The valley reclaimed, the pond was drained to the ends
Of its arms and coves to lay the parallel track,

The *parallel tracks* now lay where once lovers wooed over what was now a drained lake.

Follow the tracks as they fan out from the train station at the south end of the Train Shed.

Nineteen miles of tentacular steel track!

We have here a present view of the castle-like structure with its campanile-like tower. Before it stands the mightily sculptured Milles fountain that adorns the north entrance across Market Street. (Union Station.)

Gray stones and Spanish tiles, spires in the air,

The station's impressive ornate stone facade boasts a range of running decorative figures varying from high to very low relief. (Union Station.)

Rose over the roundhouse where the landscape ends,

This epically mythic statuary that adorns the area north of Union Station was created by the famous Swedish sculptor Carl Milles. Some in the city protested its nudity, a fact that chagrined its maker who refused to change the openness of his new figures. He did, however, consent to its name being changed to the "Meeting of the Waters."

During World War II, these passengers, mostly soldiers, wait during their time between trains. (St. Louis Public Library.)

With this view from Nineteenth Street, we can observe the 230-foot tower that looms over the massive structure. This photo was taken around the time of construction.

Here we see the tower group as they appeared together. Across Central Traffic Parkway, later known as Market Street, various businesses served Union Station passengers. (St. Louis Public Library.)

Pictured here is one of these businesses.

These surrounding shops acted as outlets for various souvenirs and trinkets associated with the station. Among these were various photo studios where visitors often posed for their pictures. Here is a 1910 photo of a traveler taken at 1819 Market Street. (Union Station.)

Two tourists sit for their picture at one of these studios.

Pictured here is another studio shot.

Here is a view of the base of the large, medieval tower and the East Pavilion.

This was the celebrated entrance to Union Station on Market Street, a *porte cochere* that was later removed when Market Street was expanded.

Here is the main entrance on Market Street.

The entrance on Eighteenth Street on the east side of this Romanesque building had rounded arches that led to the Midway, a walk area that fronted the train shed.

Since the grand station was surrounded by gaudy, cheap shops and concessions, city officials bulldozed them to improve the presence of the station. Photo *c.* 1920s. (St. Louis Public Library.)

The station provided an elegant hostel, the Terminal Hotel (pictured here *c.* 1925) for its many passengers. (St. Louis Public Library.)

As in most American cities, in March the Irish celebrate St. Patrick's Day with their annual march through downtown St. Louis. Here one such parade passes directly before Union Station on Market Street. (Union Station.)

The station as it appeared in the 1950s, surrounded by the autos and buses that in time will replace it.

Here is a view of the station's train shed as its traffic dwindled in the 1950s. In 1978, it stopped entirely. The station lay dormant after that. (Union Station.)

Pedestrians and a horse-and-buggy crowd the streets in front of the station in this early photo.

At the turn of the century, the imposing Union Station dominates the view.

Union Station, *c.* 1903, with its flow of human traffic and an electric streetcar.

Three

THE MIDWAY

Apex and terminus once of a human pool

An image taken in 1895 captures the enormous crowds that collected in the station's Midway at night. (St. Louis Public Library.)

Pictured are the entrances to the various tracks of the eighteen railroads that met here. These included those going to such far-away places as Canada, the Gulf of Mexico, and the Pacific and Atlantic coasts. (St. Louis Public Library.)

Here is another view of the Midway with trains stacked up behind the various wrought iron entrance gates. Here passengers could check their departure time and tickets as they approached their trains.

The Grand Hall acted as the principal waiting room for passengers. Of course, there was seating available throughout the entire building. Here is a shot of the elegant staircase erected in the early 1900s that led from the Grand Hall into the Midway.

One could walk directly to the Midway by using the Eighteenth Street entrance.

At one time, the station was the largest in the nation. Here is its Eighteenth Street exit.

Eighteenth Street Exit.

The Twentieth Street exit is embellished with ornamental wrought iron gates.

As seen here in this shot of the Midway in the 1940s, benches were provided for the hordes that would busily pass through the station. (St. Louis Public Library.)

Here is a view of the main lobby before remodeling took place early in the last century. It was not only noisy, but a hindrance to the main line of human traffic due to the arrangement of the seats. (St. Louis Public Library.)

After the main lobby was remodeled in the 1940s, the chairs no longer blocked floor traffic. (St. Louis Public Library.)

Here are the ticket counters as they existed in 1945 in the main lobby. (St. Louis Public Library.)

During World War II, swarms of people—many engaged in the war effort—passed through the city en route to numerous destinations. Here we see a group crowding the parcel check room in 1943–1944. (St. Louis Public Library.)

Pictured here is another look at the crowded war station. (St. Louis Public Library.)

Various concessions attracted buyers during the busy 1940s. Photo c. 1944. (St. Louis Public Library.)

GIs at the ticket counter could get a glimpse of a mural depicting the history of transportation in the city. (St. Louis Public Library.)

Here we see the hordes of military as they huddled trying to enter the gates of the Sunshine Special (St. Louis-Memphis-Texas) of the Missouri Pacific. (St. Louis Public Library.)

Two lonely passengers sit apart on the once crowded benches on the Midway in the nearly empty station in the 1970s. *That swarmed to the coupled cars with the well-oiled springs,* (St. Louis Public Library.)

Four

Train Shed, Yards, and Trains

Men armed with long poles search for vagrants. (Special Collections, St. Louis Public Library.)

Passengers at the giant station could directly enter their trains at the enormous shed which contained the various trains that they sought. Made of glass and tin, it aped many of the glass roof designs of European railroads. It was designed by George H. Pegram. Here is the large train shed as it appears from an aerial perspective. The lower left section was devoted entirely to the sorting and dispensing of mail for train delivery.

Union Station, Train Shed, St. Louis, Mo.

At the time of this photo (c. 1911), the station was one of the busiest in the nation with hundreds of trains coming in and out of St. Louis. The train shed protected the various cars and their passengers from inclement weather.

All luggage was collected in the Baggage Room and directed to the proper trains. An upstairs room was reserved for all "dead," or unclaimed, baggage.

Pictured here is the corridor, or platform, that travelers traversed to reach their trains. (Union Station.)

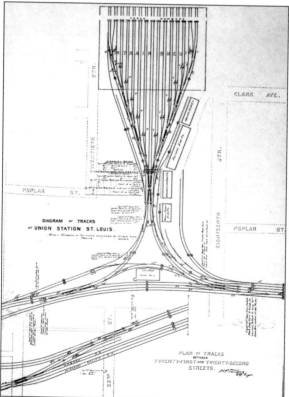

One of the major features of the yards was its powerhouse. Here various sources of energy—boiler engines, dynamos, and other devices—provided the means by which the whole operation functioned.

Link planned his schema to allow the station's tracks to end at the shed. That is, no trains ran through the city from the station. To achieve this, he envisioned trains backing into the station with no further runs. Pictured here is the manner in which the locomotives were maneuvered to back into the train shed to be in a position to leave in any direction.

This view of the train yard (c. 1911) captures not only the multiple tracks, but the intricacy of their layout.

St. Louis Union Station stands amid its 42 tracks; this number made it the largest station in the United States. As a mail carrier, it was the second largest in the nation. (St. Louis Public Library.)

An early example from 1909 illustrates how these mammoth locomotives would back their cargoes into the waiting station.

Cars of every description and every railroad are shown here in this enormous gathering of waiting trains in the terminal yards, c. 1912. Great numbers such as these went in and out of the station each day.

Of course, various models of the steam locomotive were built and utilized during these railroad years. Here is the Haenschel steam locomotive, built in Germany specifically to be used in the 1904 World's Fair.

Missouri Pacific Railroad kept introducing new models to its tracks. Here is a July 1935 picture of one such train, which became a stalwart of the line.

Pictured is an early shot of the workings of Union Station's switchyards.

One of the mammoth steam locomotives, utilized in 1912, puffs its way into the St. Louis station.

The diesel-propelled train began to appear in the 1950s, replacing the old steam models. Here we see the Texas Eagle, newly equipped with diesel capabilities, heading towards Union Station. The new fueling process quickly replaced the old steam-fitted method.

However, many of the old-fashioned sort were kept for emergency services. Here we see the popular Sunshine Special of the Missouri Pacific Line, which still in the 1940s was kept running by steam.

Cars for the Texas Eagle during April of 1977. (Skip Gatermann Collection.)

Amtrak, 1972, during the so-called "Rainbow Era" (1971–1975). (Skip Gatermann Collection.)

Engine #4501 stands in the yard in June 1970. (Skip Gatermann Collection.)

Pictured here is the Westerner #42 in April 1971. (Skip Gatermann Collection.)

Here stands MOPAC in April 1971. (Skip Gatermann Collection.)

Here is the National Limited line that runs from New York to Kansas City. It is October 29, 1978, two days before the last train will pull out of Union Station. (Skip Gatermann Collection.)

Here is an excursion by the Southern 4501 to Mt. Vernon, Illinois, in June 1970. (Skip Gatermann Collection.)

Here is another view of the 4501. (Skip Gatermann Collection.)

Here is the Cannon Ball (Norfolk and Western) in March 1970. (Skip Gatermann Collection.)

The railroads conducted constant maintenance and replacement on their passenger and freight cars. Here is one such passenger train (CB&Q, #12) being pulled from the yard on April 6, 1949. (Union Station, F. Crawford.)

Pictured here is a railroad employee working on the wheel of a steam locomotive of the 1930s. (Union Station.)

It is inconceivable that such a plant as the Union Station of 1894 could come to such an inglorious end. Nevertheless, here is a photo of the last train pulling out of Union Station on October 31, 1978. Train travel was no longer patronized by the public at large. The Railroad Age had come to its close. (Union Station.)

Five

GRAND HALL

Let us return now to September 1, 1894, when Union Station was formally opened with a blaze of glory.

This celebration marks the opening of Union Station's Grand Hall, the opulent center of the entire operation. People by the score turned out for this happy opening. With four bands and 200 musicians to entertain them, 10,000 people were invited to this grand event. (Union Station.)

Here we can witness the skill and devotion by which the interior space was put together. The arch to the right is the much vaunted "Whispering Arch." If one placed his ear on its wall on one side of the arch, someone on the other side could hear his whisper. (Union Station.)

This elaborately designed stairwell in the Grand Hall led the visitor towards the Midway and the trains.

Here is a view of one of the elaborate art pieces that adorned the Grand Hall. Culled from the mythic past, this figurine acted as one of the bearers of the Grand Hall's lights at each end of the vast interior of this large room.

Another view of the sculpted mythic figures that adorned the Grand Hall. They held up, as we can readily see, various stands of light. There were seven of these allegorical maidens who held the globed lights.

We see here the arrangement by which the windows were placed in the Grand Hall. The Greek columns support the highly decorative windows bowing in a leaning fashion to the center of the vast room. (Union Station.)

As we mount the grand staircase to the Grand Hall, we first observe the artistry of the paneled mosaic glass window that adorns the walk-up. Here we see three ornate figures etched in the glass. These represent the three railroads of New York, San Francisco, and St. Louis. St. Louis, with the old courthouse standing behind her, is the central allegorical figure.

Here we see the whispering arch entrance to the Grand Hall with the allegorical window behind it. At this point, we enter the Grand Hall.

Here is another design of rare beauty that adorns the walls of this gracious hall.

This angle of vision of the Grand Hall, as it appeared in 1911, provides us with some sense of Eastern Asia, as if there were faint traces of a Muslin mosque in this stark setting. This shot was made after the Terminal Hotel acquired the entire building as a business transaction. (Union Station.)

The Grand Hall as it appeared in the 1940s. There were other waiting rooms in this station but this area was generally used by guests who were staying at the Terminal Hotel. (Union Station.)

Six

DINING AND OTHER FACILITIES

Fred Harvey, the famed restaurateur who provided all the dining facilities for the station, is pictured here in this late nineteenth century portrait. He acquired an almost mythic reputation. Harvey started his first restaurant in St. Louis prior to the Civil War. At this site in 1896, Harvey opened the first of his many highly regarded restaurants that served the nation at large under the Harvey signature. (Union Station.)

As our previous sketch of the second floor and the location of the Grand Hall indicated, beyond the west Smoking Room ran the so-called Gothic Corridor. This passageway would lead first to the dining rooms run by the Fred Harvey management.

Here is the elegant entrance to the major restaurant of the building. The dining room itself was such a favorite with its top cuisine that many of the locals—as well as travelers—ate there.

Here is a view of the restaurant with its elaborate place settings and other arty items that decorate the ornate wall and ceiling. (Union Station.)

In 1930, the Fred Harvey Chain added another dining hall to its list of eateries at the station. The Lunch Room was located on the Midway across from the train shed. It was served by the so-called Harvey Girls, who in their perky uniforms prettily provided the service at various counters and tables. (Union Station.)

Here is the famed Fred Harvey Restaurant. (St. Louis Public Library.)

Part of the staff at the Fred Harvey restaurants were the hardy bread makers, pictured here in the 1940s. (Union Station, Lona Griffin.)

In addition to the major restaurant off the Gothic Corridor, there were many opulent, private dining rooms run by the firm. Here is one such room with a western view of its interior.

Here is a look from the east at another view of the elegant setting of furniture and art objects that filled a private dining room.

The Ladies Waiting Room was reserved for ladies only, and was also equipped with a nursery of sorts where the care and tending of babies and small toddlers could take place.

There was a sense of grace and elegance that pervaded the Ladies Waiting Room that provided it with an air of serenity and sanctuary.

As we can see here, the room contained many objects of great beauty, such as the figure adorning the mantel of this exquisite fireplace.

The room was filled with spacious aisles and comfortable chairs.

The general waiting room on the ground floor was right off the Midway near the ticket offices.

As we have noted, during World War II every serviceman of any stripe or color seemed to have passed through Union Station. Here we see a soldier and a sailor being shown some text at the Fred Harvey Book Store in 1944. (St. Louis Public Library.)

Seven

OPERATIONS

The operational means by which this large complex was able to handle as many as 100,000 passengers a day was an engineering and technological triumph. Safety, of course, was a primary concern. The principal aim was to prevent any sort of collision on the station's many tracks. There were occasional accidents, as when one train jumped its tracks and crashed headlong into the train shed itself. But on the whole there were very few. This was due to the ingenuity of the technical and operational devices with which the station was equipped, as this chapter will illustrate.

The Station Master's office carefully scrutinized the arrival and departure of trains. The building stood facing the Midway on one side and the tracks on the other. The building contained a telegraph office, a bulletin board announcing train schedules, and the clock tower.

Another important factor in conducting traffic was the switch room located in the powerhouse in the train yards. As the nerve center of the entire operation, the center contained boilers, dynamos, and engines that powered the communication and other systems.

Within the powerhouse is located the interlocking machine, which sent electricity and power to the entire operation. All switching movements of the trains in the yards were controlled through this center by the director in charge.

At each end of the individual tracks in the train shed, various bumpers ("The Avenue of the Bumpers") were placed to receive the jolts of the entering trains.

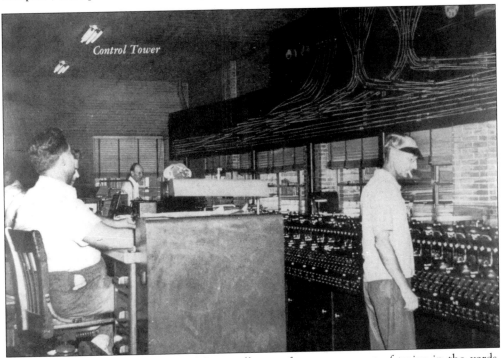

Control Tower

Switch tower staff conducted careful surveillance of any movement of trains in the yards. Any engineer moving his train must be guided by the director of the tower. Photo *c.* 1944. (St. Louis Public Library.)

The Telegraph Service was an early accommodation for the traveler. Here we see an early staff conducting its business.

All reservations were made and finalized in this, the reservation section of the Station. The date is 1945. (St. Louis Public Library.)

Eight

SUBURBAN STATIONS

We return now to the early rail routes in St. Louis with an emphasis on the substations, depots, shelters, and even whistle stops that grew up around them. As we do, we must not in any manner ignore the rise of the so-called "interurban" commuter trains that began to appear in the area. These "accommodation trains" were introduced by the early railroads to service the various townships and hamlets that were growing up in St. Louis and St. Charles Counties. As populations in these nearby towns grew, more and more trains were needed to service the hordes of people who were living in these places, and who were working in downtown St. Louis. Later, these special trains would be dubbed the "Comms," and became for decades the transportation of numerous people coming into St. Louis from such stops as Kirkwood, Webster Groves, Ferguson, and dozens of others. However, our emphasis here will remain on the buildings that housed their connecting points. Again in making this leap backward into time, it would be best to recall that many of these suburban stations existed long before Union Station and some before the Depot that preceded it.

Here, in what is now a custard shop and a railroad museum, stands an early version of the Ferguson station. This building, once in decline after the railroads' closing of all commuter traffic, was handsomely restored by the town's historical society. This small track-side depot is the only one remaining in Missouri in the Wabash pattern. Photo: turn of the twentieth century. (Ferguson Historical Society.)

The Ferguson depot was host to many community functions such as church services (1867), voting facilities, and once even a telegraph office. A crowd of commuters waits for their St. Louis connection in the late nineteenth century. (Ferguson Historical Society.)

Here we see anticipation mounting as an engine is at last spotted nearing the Ferguson Station. (Ferguson Historical Society.)

An engineer named Hilbert poses in the cab of an old Wabash engine before 1894. This train, en route to the Ferguson station, was one of many others that served that community. (Ferguson Historical Society.)

Around 1885, there was no trestle at Florissant Road, a major artery through the town. A trestle was later built here and then rebuilt in 1937. The tracks belonged to the Wabash railroad. (Ferguson Historical Society.)

Ferguson Station today is "The Whistle Stop," a frozen-custard business.

Here is another railroad substation in Ferguson. Called the Darst Station, it is shown here in all of its pioneer exuberance: a man hunting with his dog, shooting from the tracks. (Ferguson Historical Society.)

Here is the St. Charles Depot as it existed in those early days when trains were carried across the wide Missouri on barges. There was no Missouri bridge at that time.

Here is the O'Fallon country train station. (Skip Gatermann Collection.)

Our next stop is Kirkwood, which is one of the stations that remains open to this day. There was train service to Kirkwood as early as 1853. The first station was a primitive wooden affair. It was replaced in 1863 by another frame building. The graceful train station that still stands today was constructed in 1893.

With this 1938 sign, we can see how the railroads would advertise their service. Standing next to this railroad security tower is a sign promising a ride on the Missouri Pacific Lines for a moderate price. (Francis Scheidegger.)

Depicted here is the so-called "Round House" of the Kirkwood MOPAC tracks in 1940 where locomotives were being turned around by crew members for their return trips to St. Louis. (Kirkwood Historical Society.)

This is a present-day shot of the Kirkwood Station as its customers wait for the Amtrak system which, as we well know, inherited the train business after its great decline.

A stream-lined train approaches the Kirkwood Station in the present day. It is, of course, an Amtrak train.

A train arrives at the Kirkwood Station.

Built in 1891, this station served the Meramec Highlands Resort that became a rather popular gathering place for people coming to St. Louis during the World's Fair in 1904. Later it became the Osage Hills Depot. It is now deserted and threatened with demolition.

On the grounds of the National Museum of Transportation is preserved this old tunnel which once was used by trains coming into town.

This station, called the Woodlawn Station, was built in 1910. It was then called the Woodlawn Station of Kirkwood, and it was torn down in 1952.

Webster Groves was provided with several rail stops, a few of which we picture below. Here is an early station—simple in its structure—that exists on Big Bend Blvd.

The old station on Gore Avenue is now occupied by Faith Academy of Montessori.

Here is another Webster Groves station, certainly more posh than the others previously pictured. It must have been built to live up to its name, "Tuxedo Park Station."

This Victorian Webster Groves Station in the 1800s captures with great authenticity the architecture and the clothing of the times. It was called the Elwood Station.

One of the better known thoroughfares is Old Orchard Avenue. Here we see its early railroad station.

Commuters could (if they hurried) catch the trains at Lake Junction, a flag stop, near Summit and Pacific.

Here is Pacific Station (c. 1896). The first railroad established in the city was the Pacific, which built the first tracks from Pacific to St. Louis. In this photo we see a train being conducted into the Pacific area, whose engineer was a man named Mr. Kelly. (Meramec Valley Historical Society.)

To continue our survey, we must look into the neighboring state of Illinois, for rail traffic from that area began as early as that in Missouri. This station, which is still active, is located in Alton, Illinois.

Here is the Edwardsville Norfolk Western Station. (Skip Gatermann Collection.)

Pictured here is the depot in Waterloo, Illinois, owned by Gulf, Mobile, and Ohio. (Skip Gatermann Collection.)

Delmar Station, one of two stations in St. Louis that provided its citizenry with a great deal of comfort in years past. It stands here today, a classical structure of great historical significance.

Here is an image of Bremen station, which once carried Cardinal baseball players as they went to and fro to the old Sportsmen Park in North St. Louis. (Skip Gatermann Collection.)

McKinley Terminal in downtown St. Louis was named after Senator William McKinley, a U.S. Senator from Danville, Illinois.

Notice that the freight at Wabash Freight Station, St. Louis, 1906, is carried by horse-drawn wagons.

Nine

POSTCARDS

Central to the cultural and entertainment life of the circle surrounding St. Louis, both in Missouri and Illinois, is, of course, the city itself. One of its grand features, then and now, is present and past Union Station. With its rebirth as a great entertainment center with concessions and shops, theatres and hotels, the station offers many sorts of present-day postcards. Not as many, however, as the old station did. Here are a few examples of the postcards that were sold throughout the years.

This is a contemporary card depicting the splashy waters of the famous "Meeting of the Water" statuary of the Milles fountain.

As the legend explains under the postcard, the IC railroad provided excursions to various cities in Illinois from St. Louis. (Postcard *c.* 1910.)

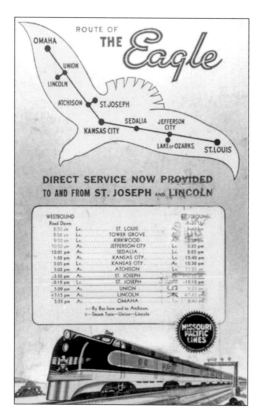

The famous "Eagle" is here marked out for its route from St. Louis to Omaha (1940). The Eagle was one of the most admired trains of its day because of its speed.

United War Fund — USO Lounge,
Union Station, Indianapolis, Ind.

At ease in the USO Lounge,
Union Station, Terre Haute, Ind.

Corner of USO Lounge,
Pennsylvania Station, Logansport, Ind.

USO Lounge,
Union Station, St. Louis, Mo.

As this photocard readily indicates, to provide R&R for World War II service men, various USOs were established. Here are multiple shots of military men entertaining themselves in their lounge in Union Station.

Union Station, St. Louis

Royal Gorge

Mormon Temple, Salt Lake City

Burlington Route Through Train

THE BURLINGTON'S PERSONALLY CONDUCTED TOURIST EXCURSIONS—THROUGH SCENIC COLORADO AND SALT LAKE CITY IN DAYLIGHT—ARE THE POSITIVELY IDEAL, CARE-FREE AND ECONOMICAL WAY TO GO TO CALIFORNIA.

Behold: the route of the Burlington Railroad's guided tour from the Midwest to California. (Postcard dated 1910.)

Hurrah! Here is Union Station, alive and kicking in the midst of its bright new station.

Union Station—St. Louis, Mo. *Greetings from St Louis M. Heith...*

This card, dated 1907, captures the monumental Union Station as it appears in its full-

June 5th .06

309. UNION STATION, ST. LOUIS. CENTRAL BAHNHOF.

This card, dated June 5, 1906, was sent by someone whose initials appear to be WJD.

UNION STATION AT NIGHT, ST. LOUIS, MO.—12

Union Station caught at night in a blaze of lights.

Market Street opens up as a grand vista to embrace the Old Court House at its beginning, and Union Station and Aloe Plaza at its end.

Again a shot of the massive station; this time, however, it's upstaged by a series of lights (probably Christmas lights) glistening before it on Aloe Plaza.

Here is the front side of a Union Station card, dated 1910.

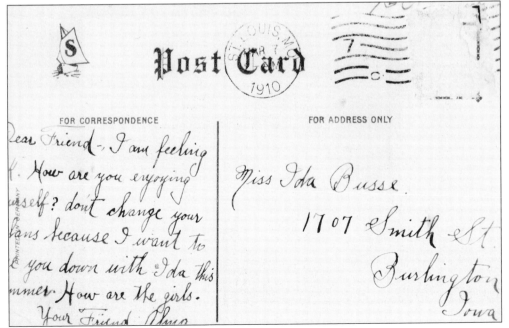

Here is the back side of this same card.

UNION STATION, ST. LOUIS, MISSOURI, SHOWING PLAZA AND FOUNTAINS

Union Station in 1943 with its distinguished plaza and fountain.

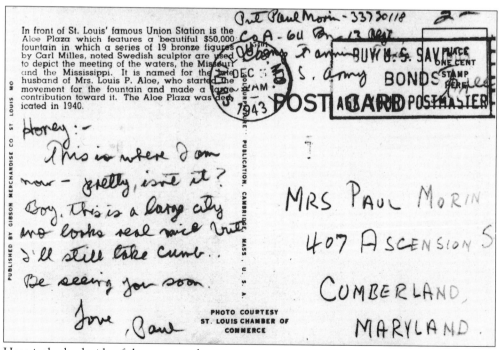

In front of St. Louis' famous Union Station is the Aloe Plaza which features a beautiful $50,000 fountain in which a series of 19 bronze figures by Carl Milles, noted Swedish sculptor are used to depict the meeting of the waters, the Missouri and the Mississippi. It is named for the husband of Mrs. Louis P. Aloe, who started the movement for the fountain and made a large contribution toward it. The Aloe Plaza was dedicated in 1940.

PUBLISHED BY GIBSON MERCHANDISE CO ST. LOUIS MO

PUBLICATION, CAMBRIDGE, MASS., U.S.A.

PHOTO COURTESY
ST. LOUIS CHAMBER OF
COMMERCE

Honey :—

This is where I am now — pretty, isn't it? Boy, this is a large city and looks real nice but I'll still take Cumb.. Be seeing you soon.

Love, Paul

DEC 1943

BUY U.S. SAV
BONDS
POST CARD

Mrs Paul Morin
407 Ascension S
Cumberland,
Maryland

Here is the back side of the same card.

Ten

DECLINE AND A NEW BEGINNING

As we have often reported, Union Station went into a vast decline in the 1950s and 1960s as rail traffic dropped to a trickle. It stopped entirely at Union Station in 1978 as most people refused to utilize the trains at all. Generations sprang up that had never been on a train. Finally, Union Station was abandoned, and to the great dismay of the city, descended into a state of disrepair and decline. Where once had been a jewel of the city, it now had become its sore.

The once-opulent station had become a shambles of cracked and fallen walls, and dirt-littered floors. (Union Station.)

Where rolling stock stands here rusting in silence.

The famed Terminal Hotel faced its terminal end.

The town did not altogether desert this treasure and through the years sought a developer. Finally, a New York firm, Oppenheimer Properties, accepted the challenge and spent $150 million on its restoration. The famous local firm of Hellmuth, Obata, and Kassabaum was selected as the architect, along with The Rouse Co. The developers and a whole army of workers, designers, and engineers labored for years to bring it back to its original graceful state. Months of painstaking detailed and exacting attention were paid to every feature to call back its original beauty. (Jefferson National Expansion Memorial, NPS.)

Here, city and state officials attend the grand opening of the renewed station. (Union Station.)

Finally, in the summer of 1985, the project was finished. Its grand opening in August was attended by thousands as they crowded the station to listen to such noted politicians as then governor, John Ashcroft. He is shown here as he holds a pick to drive in a golden spike to the restored rail tracks. (Union Station.)

Pictured here, an array of VIPs gathers to honor the opening of the new Union Station on August 29, 1985. (Union Station.)

A huge merry crowd thronged the sidewalks and entrance halls with their shouts of welcome as the station opened that August day. (Union Station.)

Pictured here is a group of Union Station workers. (Union Station.)

To honor the grand opening, Union Pacific sent in Engine #951 to celebrate the event. (Skip Gatermann Collection.)

Union Pacific's steam locomotive, Norfolk and Western Y6A 2156, being brought into the station for the grand opening. (Union Station.)

Anheuser Busch's tourist trolley came in to add to the performance of "Meet Me in St. Louis," given as a street presentation. (Union Station.)

This promotional photo featuring a smiling, welcoming conductor attempts to sway a new generation to start using the reopened station for their entertainment. (Union Station.)

Eleven

RENOVATED FACILITIES AND AMUSEMENTS

Here, in all of its distinctive beauty, is the laboriously restored Grand Hall. Not only does it serve as the aesthetic center and heart of the entire restored Union Station, but also as the brilliant lobby of the Hyatt Regency Hotel.

Pictured here is a closer view of the various accoutrements that comfort visitors as they enter. There are fanciful Victorian lights, palms, and seats that take one back to the original station.

The hall bedecked in its decorative splendor.

Another view of the Grand Hall reveals the ornate entrance to the reopened hotel.

The Victorians loved greenery in their surroundings. Here we see a modern attempt to recapture some of that effect in the plants lined up in this chamber.

A view of the barrel-wall ceiling restored to its original appearance. (Union Station.)

Off to the east of the Grand Hall is the arched entrance to an area now used as offices.

Here is a shot of the Midway as it appears after the restoration. (Union Station.)

A great crush of people advance upon the line of shops on the Midway. From this photo, we can gauge the huge popularity of this venue. (Union Station.)

Here is another view of the Midway with its central open space, where a small stream is located amidst some plants. Behind this arrangement is the center's clock.

The Midway leading to the train shed. The two blend, as we can see, providing the visitor with any sort of shop for food or clothing.

Here we are able to observe the new Midway and train shed

The old train shed is now converted into a plethora of eateries. Here one can enjoy, in picnic fashion, ethnic food of most sorts. These are provided by small shops that line the concourse. (Union Station.)

At this spot, we can observe customers eating various ethnic foods at a giant dining area that many of the shops support. (Union Station.)

Another view of the train shed and its upper area, where food is served to countless visitors who have come this time not for departure, but for fun.

Communal tables are scattered about the culinary section of this area.

The first hotel built during the restoration was the Omni. In time, it was replaced by the Hyatt Regency which continues to operate it.

Here is the green balcony area of some of the rooms in the Hyatt Regency Hotel.

The hotel's lavish veranda with its rattan chairs offers a look that may be associated with the spa hotels of the nineteenth century.

Lest we not forget, here is a bountifully equipped National Museum of Transportation exhibit with rows of miniature cars. (Union Station.)

Here is "the hottest ticket in town," the concession, where chocolate is deliciously prepared and demonstrated in a little cameo show.

Pictured here is the Midway and shops.

Again we see the Midway with more shops.

A father and his child watch in fascination as a clown creates various figures with blown-up balloons.

Union Station constantly features various entertainments for tourists who flock to its doors. Here, a buffalo soldier reenacts his role as a serviceman in the Far West. (Union Station.)

Twelve

"A New Life Springs"

Our chronology of the life and times of Union Station ends with a close look at the miracle of reconstruction that the massive building underwent to recover its old dignity and grace.

Here is a gigantic sign announcing the presence of the station. It looms over the area where once the gates to the trains stood.

To the layman, the train shed is the most spectacular part of the new restoration. The shed area has been converted into a parking lot, surrounded by play areas for kids.

A view of one of the station's most spectacular features: its small lake overlooked by the luxury hotel, the Hyatt Regency. The lake is alive with paddle-boats and ducks.

Here are various tent concessions that sell everything from jewels to souvenirs. (Union Station.)

Attendants here "tend the store" under one of the tent concessions. (Union Station.)

Here is one of the many theatricals held under the giant roof: Irish dancers on St. Patrick's Day. (Union Station.)

Here is another group of actors in a presentation under the train shed. (Union Station.)

Within the train yards stands the popular Hard Rock Café.

The YMCA hotel, which once housed post office workers who sorted mail on the trains, is now the Drury Inn, a popular hotel.

The old Post Office Annex has now been renovated and turned into a suite of offices. Formerly, it was used for the processing of mail for the trains.

In the lace of a trestle and track,

. . . a sunken pool,

Honeysuckle hangs in the air:

a new life springs.

Bibliography

Barnes, Harper. *Standing on a Volcano*. St. Louis, Missouri: Missouri Historical Society, 2001.

Bartholomew, Harland and Associates. *Down by the Gravois*. St. Louis, Missouri, 1976.

Byerby, Barbara J. and Lester, J.B. *Kirkwood, Missouri, The Green Tree City*. St. Louis, Missouri: Webster-Kirkwood Times, Inc., 1994.

Christensen et al. *Dictionary of Missouri Biography*. Columbia, Missouri: University of Missouri Press, 1999.

Eliot, T.S. *Poems and Plays (1909–1950)*. New York, New York: Harcourt Brace, 1971.

Ferguson Historical Society. *Ferguson: A City and Its People*. Ferguson, Missouri, 1976.

Grant H. Roger et al. *St. Louis Union Station*. St. Louis Mercantile Library, 1994.

Guenther, Charles. "Union Station." St. Louis, Missouri: Nevertheless Press, 1983. (Poem used by permission of the author.)

Hubbard, Howard. *Masterpieces of Western Sculpture*. New Jersey: Chatwell Books, 1966.

Parker, Edward C. *Next Stop: St. Louis Union Station*. St. Louis, Missouri: Patrice Press, 1989.

Rehkopf, Charles. *Pictorial History of Webster Groves, Missouri*. Webster Groves, Missouri: Webster-Kirkwood Times, Inc., 1991.

Terminal Railroad Association of St. Louis. *Fifty Years of Transportation: St. Louis Station and St. Louis*. St. Louis, Missouri, 1941.

Wayman, Norbury. *St. Louis Union Station and Its Railroads*. St. Louis, Missouri: Evelyn. E. Newman Group, 1986.

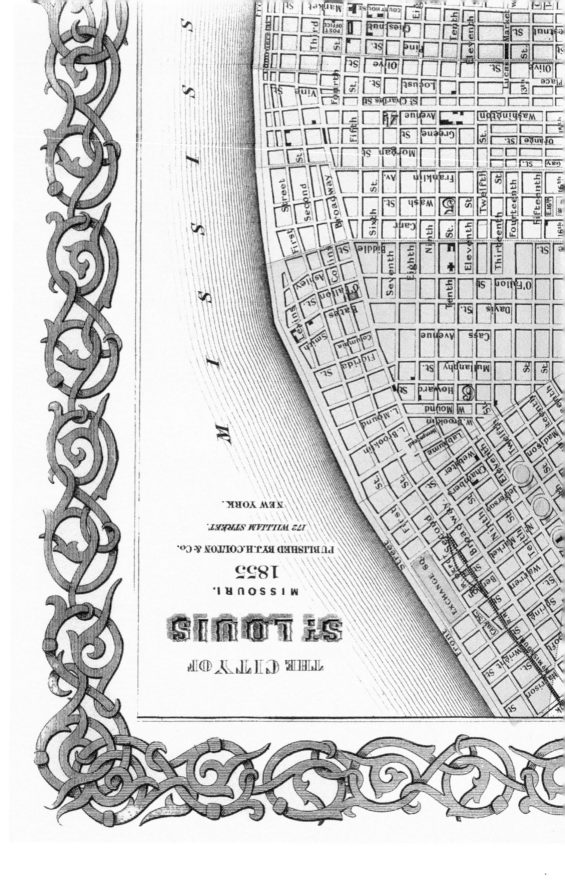

THE CITY OF
ST LOUIS
MISSOURI.

1855

PUBLISHED BY J.H.COLTON & Co.

172 WILLIAM STREET.

NEW YORK.

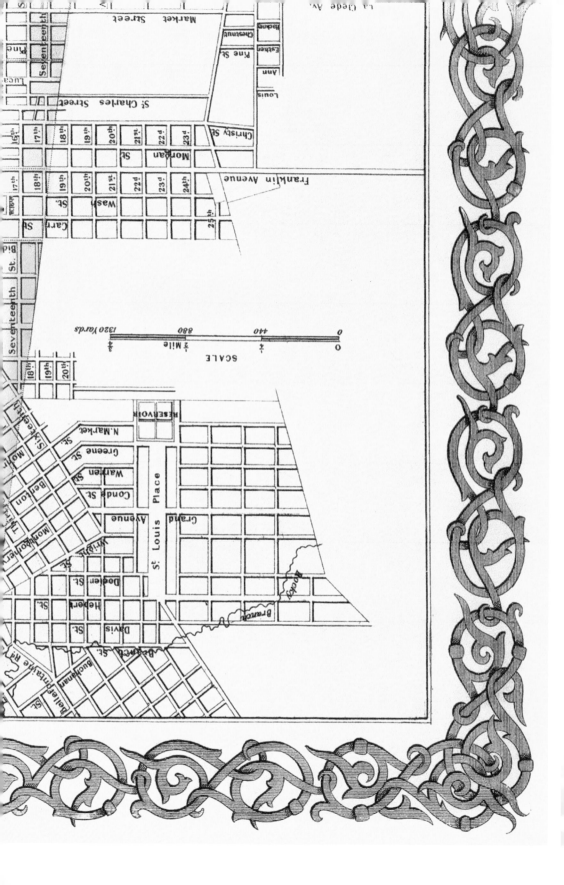